This journal belongs to:

....

I pray that the God who gives hope will fill you with much joy and peace while you trust in him. Then your hope will overflow by the power of the Holy Spirit.

Romans 15:13

Give me back the *joy*
that comes when you save me.
Keep me strong by giving me a willing spirit.

Psalm 51:12

I have obeyed my Father's commands, and I remain in his love. In the same way, if you obey my commands, you will remain in my love. I have told you these things so that you can have the same joy I have. I want your joy to be the fullest joy.

John 15:10–11

But the Spirit gives love, joy, peace, patience, kindness, goodness, faithfulness, gentleness, self-control. There is no law that says these things are wrong.

Galatians 5:22–23

Heavens and earth, be happy.
Mountains, shout with joy.
Be happy because the Lord comforts his people.
He will comfort those who suffer.

Isaiah 49:13

What were the earth's foundations set on? Or who put its cornerstone in place? Who did all this while the morning stars sang together? Who did this while the angels shouted with *joy*?

Job 38:6–7

You are happy when people hate you and are cruel to you. You are happy when they say that you are evil because you belong to the Son of Man. At that time be full of joy, because you have a great reward in heaven.

Luke 6:22–23

Lord, you have made me happy by what you have done. I will sing for joy about what your hands have done.

Psalm 92:4

The joy of the Lord
will make you strong.

Nehemiah 8:10

I tell you the truth.
You will cry and be sad,
but the world will be happy.
You will be sad, but your sadness
will become joy.

John 16:20

Serve the Lord with **joy**.
Come before him with singing.

Psalm 100:2

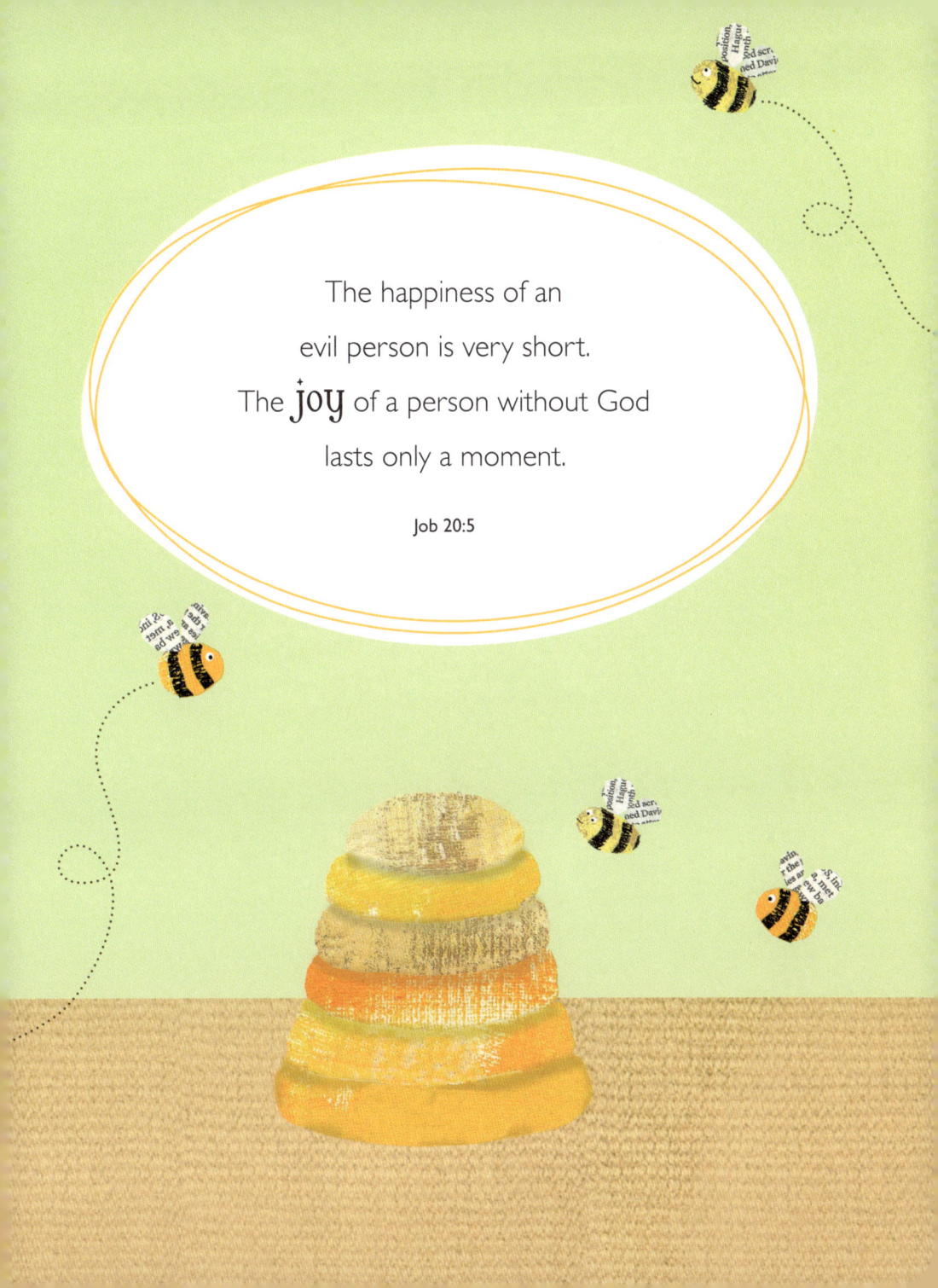

Sing a new song to him.
Play well and **joyfully**.

Psalm 33:3

And we also have **joy** with our troubles because we know that these troubles produce patience.

Romans 5:3

There is a river which
brings joy to the city of God.
This is the holy place
where God Most High lives.

Psalm 46:4

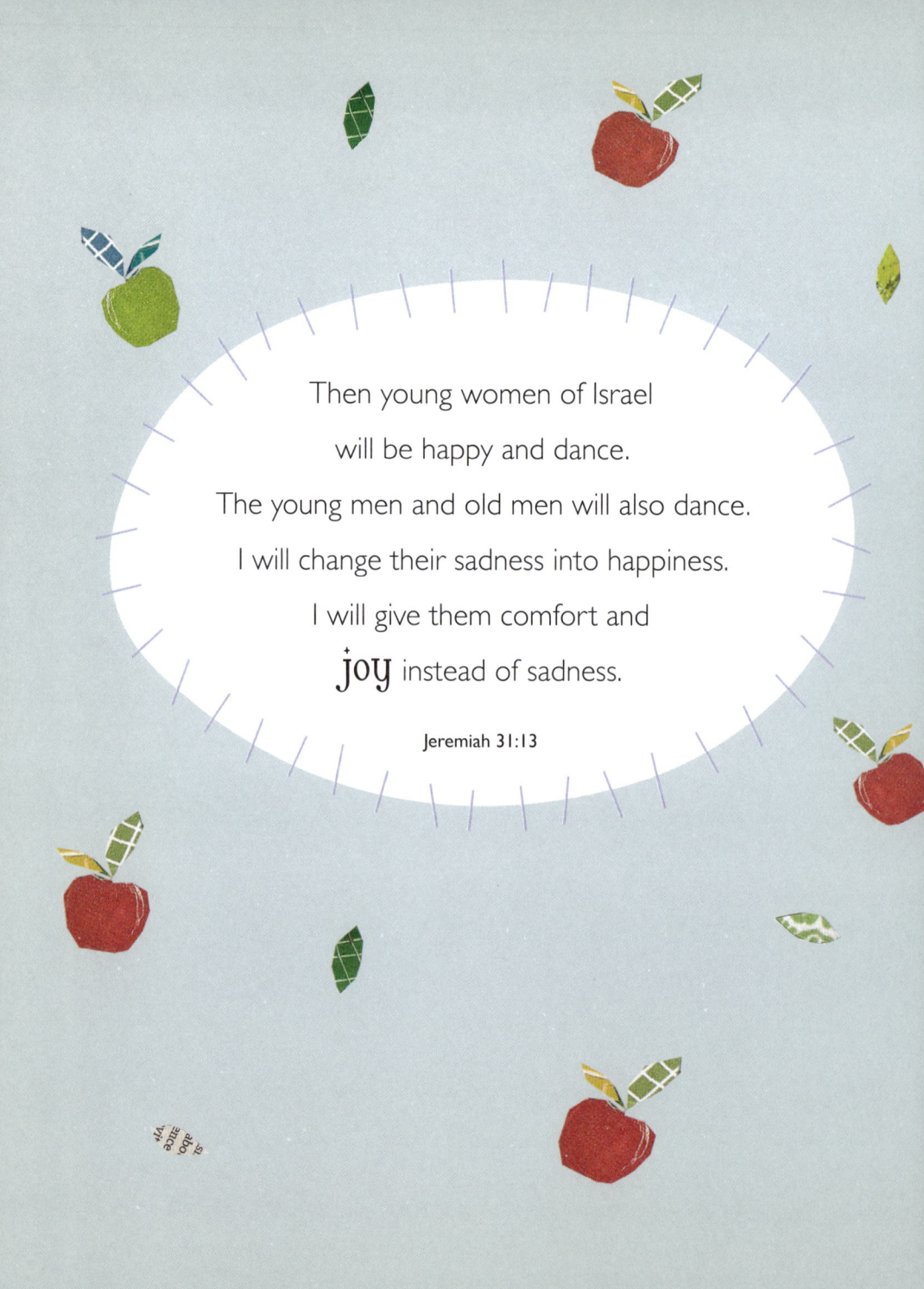

I will shout for joy

when I sing praises to you.

You have saved me.

Psalm 71:23

You people who are now hungry are happy, because you will be satisfied. You people who are now crying are happy, because you will laugh with joy.

Luke 6:21

It is the same with you. Now you are sad. But I will see you again and you will be happy. And no one will take away your joy.

John 16:22

The Lord has filled my heart with joy.

I feel very strong in the Lord.

I can laugh at my enemies.

I am glad because you have helped me!

1 Samuel 2:1

In the same way, I tell you there is much joy in heaven when one sinner changes his heart. There is more joy for that one sinner than there is for ninety-nine good people who don't need to change.

Luke 15:7

May my friends sing and shout for joy.

May they always say,

"Praise the greatness of the Lord.

He loves to see his servants do well."

Psalm 35:27

Light shines on those who do right.
Joy belongs to those who are honest.

Psalm 97:11

Obey your leaders and be under their authority. These men are watching you because they are responsible for your souls. Obey them so that they will do this work with **joy**, not sadness. It will not help you to make their work hard.

Hebrews 13:17

You have not seen Christ, but still you love him.
You cannot see him now, but you believe in him.
You are filled with a *joy* that cannot be explained.
And that joy is full of glory.

1 Peter 1:8

God is strong and can help you not to fall. He can bring you before his glory without any wrong in you and give you great *joy*.

Jude 24

The angel said to them, "Don't be afraid, because I am bringing you some good news. It will be a *joy* to all the people. Today your Savior was born in David's town. He is Christ, the Lord."

Luke 2:10–11

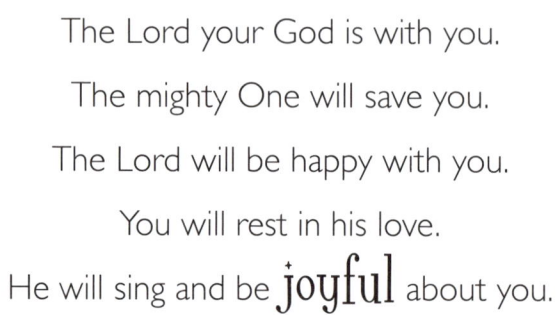

The Lord your God is with you.
The mighty One will save you.
The Lord will be happy with you.
You will rest in his love.
He will sing and be *joyful* about you.

Zephaniah 3:17

God gives the lonely a home.

He leads prisoners out with *joy*.

Psalm 68:6

If one has the gift of encouraging others, he should encourage. If one has the gift of giving to others, he should give freely. If one has the gift of being a leader, he should try hard when he leads. If one has the gift of showing kindness to others, that person should do so with joy.

Romans 12:8

My brothers, be full of *joy* in the Lord.

Philippians 3:1